Sept. 17
1996
Grandma
From
Benjamin

Kwitchyerbellyakin

and other bits and pieces
of everyday living

by Debbie Pendergast
Illustrated by Jaynie R. Gibson

Third Printing • November 1995

Library of Congress Catalog Card Number: 94-93924
ISBN 1-885591-36-5

Some of these stories have appeared previously in
Florida Today and *The Coalfield Progress*.

Additional copies are available. For your convenience, an order
form
can be found at the back of this book.

Printed in the USA by
Morris Publishing
3212 East Hwy 30 • Kearney, NE 68847

This book is dedicated with love and gratitude
to Scotty, Ginny, and Megan
dp

To my family with all my love
jg

ACKNOWLEDGMENTS

I would like to thank my wonderful family and friends who so graciously allowed me to use their real names in this book. I would also like to thank the following people for the special role they played in making this book a reality:

Louella Benton for being my daughters' wonderful teacher and my wonderful friend.

Julie Evans for her computer wisdom.

Janeen Merrill for her constant encouragement to keep writing.

Monroe Moore, my daddy, for all his remarkable bits of advice.

Alice Marie Pendergast, my sister-in-law and English teacher at Smoky Mountain High School, for her extraordinary editing skills.

John and Helen Pendergast, Mom and Dad, for their faith in me.

Sue Rife for her endless patience in listening to these stories over and over.

Sue Sturgill for her unfaltering friendship and unique PR skills.

I am truly blessed to have you all in my life.

♥ CONTENTS ♥

KWITCHYERBELLYAKIN

Visitors always express an interest in our oblong, cross stitch sampler above the pantry: Kwitchyerbellyakin.

"What does that say?"

"Sound out the letters."

"I don't think it really says anything. Kwitch, kwitch yer...is this some of your southern dialect? Kwitch–yer–belly–a–kin. Oh, that's it! Kwitchyerbellyakin. What does that mean?"

"Just what it says—don't feel sorry for yourself."

"That's neat. Where did you get it?"

I smile and say, "My mother made it."

Now that's a simple answer to a simple question, but HOW I finally got the sampler framed and hanging in my kitchen is a little more complicated.

My mother enjoyed crocheting and cross stitching, but she didn't have much free time back in the early seventies. She was busy working full time and raising a family.

1

That was before February 1971 when my mother, at age forty-seven, suffered a massive heart attack. I was only sixteen at the time and I felt my world had collapsed. There was a long hospital stay and finally, Mother got to come home. She was still very weak, but she wanted something to do, so she brought out her needlework.

One afternoon I was complaining in my usual self-pitying way about not being able to buy a special pair of shoes I wanted.

"I really need those shoes, Mother."

She put her needlework aside and said, "You have plenty of shoes now. If you want them that badly then save your money. Remember, 'I once cried because I had no shoes till I saw a man who had no feet.'"

I hated when she used that line on me. It was supposed to make me feel guilty which it usually did, but it also made me angry.

"Debbie..." I turned to look at her and she was sitting there with a big smile holding her finished cross stitch piece.

"Well, what is that supposed to say?" I asked impatiently.

"Something I want you to remember all your life—Kwitchyerbellyakin—which means stop feeling sorry for yourself, count your blessings, be happy." She laughed as she got up to give me a big hug.

It was impossible to stay mad at her.

My mother passed away in June of that year—another heart attack. I lost my best friend in the whole world and I didn't realize it until she was gone.

In the grief-filled days that followed, I absently packed away many of Mother's things, including the sampler, the last cross stitch she had done.

Years passed and I must admit that I forgot all about the sampler. We were getting ready for a move to Florida and my cousin was helping us clean the attic.

"What do you want me to do with these?" she asked as she held up some old boxes.

"Oh, just take them with you and I'll go through them when we come in next year. I don't have the energy to look through any more boxes."

Several weeks passed and by this time we were situated (almost) in a small duplex in Central Florida. It was not my idea of home. I missed our family, our friends, and our house. I was in the midst of a real swinging pity party when the doorbell rang. It was the UPS man with a thin, oblong package from my cousin.

When I opened it I couldn't believe my eyes! There was my mother's sampler all pressed and framed and speaking to me as clearly as it had on that first day—Kwitchyerbellyakin!

I sat down and cried; not only because I was so happy to receive this wonderful gift, but because my mother would never know how much it meant to me—and still does.

When we moved into our new home several years ago, I hung the sampler in the kitchen where everyone could see it and be reminded, in the words of a very wise and wonderful woman, to KWITCHYERBELLYAKIN!

THE THREE BEST MINUTES

I saw the two small figures long before they saw me. Dragging their backpacks behind them and deep in conversation, they made their way down the sidewalk.

"Did you have a nice day at school?" I asked as Megan and her friend, Jackie, got a little closer.

"Yes," came the unison reply.

As Megan walked past me to the door, she turned and said in a nonchalant way, "I won second place in a poster contest."

"Oh, that's ....", but before I could finish she and Jackie had headed off to play.

At dinner Megan again mentioned her second place win and we all gave her a hearty round of congratulations. She didn't seem too excited.

That night, after reading stories and saying prayers, I told Megan that I was very proud of her second place win.

Her little eyes lit up and she said, "Oh Mommy, I wanted to talk about it this afternoon, but I didn't want to sound braggy in front of Jackie."

"I'm glad," I commented with a smile.

"But Mommy, it was so neat! They called the winners' names over the loudspeaker and I was just sitting there not thinking I would win. Then they called my name and EVERYONE in my class clapped for me. It was the best minute of my life."

I started to speak, but Megan quickly continued...

"And then, Mommy, I was the first person in my class to finish all the math facts and EVERYONE clapped for me again. It was the second best minute of my life.

"And then, Mommy, I finally got up to sing about the presidents in order and I got them all right. EVERYONE clapped for me again! It was the third best minute of my life."

She gave me a big hug and exclaimed, "Oh, Mommy, I've had the three best minutes of my life today. I'm so happy."

"And I'm so happy for you," I said as I tucked her in bed.

When I closed her door I thought about Megan's "three best minutes." According to Andy Warhol, she's due for at least twelve more minutes in the limelight.

If those twelve minutes are anything like her first three, she will live a charmed life, indeed.

We should all be so lucky.

A NOT-SO-PERFECT FAMILY

"I think you all are the perfect family."

My friend's comment startled me. For an instant I wanted to thank her and bask in the glow of the compliment, but instead I blurted, "Whatever gave you THAT idea?"

She smiled and said, "Well, you all seem pretty perfect to me. You do things together and you all seem to get along."

This perception of perfection was a dangerous thing. No family could live up to it—mine included.

My friend was partially right, we do try to do things together. However, there is usually an argument from someone about anything we try to do.

Going for a walk together sounds like a simple little family outing, but in this household there is nothing simple.

"Come on, let's all go for a walk."

The nine-year-old wants to ride her bike instead of walking. The fourteen-year-old thinks it's too hot to walk and whines that we should just drive.

By the time everyone gets started, the nine-year-old is running ahead of us and the fourteen-year-old is lagging behind us hoping no one will notice that she's out walking with "her parents"!

When we get back home the nine-year-old is aggravated because she had to keep circling the block to find us, the fourteen-year-old is grouchy because she is sweaty and her hair has flopped, my husband says the next time he's going to walk by himself, and I worry that the four of us can't take a simple walk without someone complaining.

Perfect? Hardly!

We do go to church together, but again, if my friend could see behind the scenes, her opinion would probably change.

My husband and I are up bright and early on Sunday morning. Our fourteen-year-old begs to sleep "for another hour or so" while her nine-year-old sister is "at a really good part in this book."

"Too bad," we say, "we're going to church."

The fourteen-year-old comes out of her room with shorts on and a wrinkled shirt. I take one look and tell her to go change. She insists she has nothing else clean. I say fine. Put on a dirty dress. An argument usually follows.

As we are about to get in the van, we realize the nine-year-old is not with us. My husband goes to check and discovers she is reading that "good part" in her book, still dressed in her pajamas!

My husband tells her to get dressed NOW so she waltzes out to the van in shorts.

On the way to church the fourteen-year-old argues that it isn't fair that her sister is wearing shorts while she has to wear a dirty dress. Her sister argues that it isn't fair that she had to stop reading "at the best part" in her book. My husband argues that it isn't fair that we have to listen to all this commotion, especially on Sunday. I argue that they all better behave in church or they'll pay later. So much for the perfect family.

I wonder what my friend would think if she could see us all on our not-so-perfect days.

For my husband it would be those lousy days at work that he brings home with him. The girls and I wonder why he bites our heads off when we ask a simple question, but then we all exchange a knowing glance and I ask, "Oh, bad day at work?"

My answer is usually an affirmative grunt.

The fourteen-year-old is in the midst of a Holy Hormone War which means her moods vary greatly. Her not-so-perfect days usually begin in the morning before school starts when she decides she is having a bad hair day and nothing in her closet is fit to wear.

The nine-year-old is relatively easy going (remember, she has not hit adolescence); however, she can turn into a real whiner when her play time is interrupted by the reminder that she has to leave for piano lessons.

On my not-so-perfect days when I feel my family does not appreciate ALL I do for them, I choose to wear my Martyred Mother Look. It is not highly effective, but I continue anyway hoping that someday one of them will notice and spend the rest of their lives thanking me for all the wonderful things I have done.

For all our not-so-perfect days and ways, we do manage to have some moments, however brief, of near perfection.

There are those moments when we're all watching a family movie with a big bowl of popcorn to share. No one is arguing, complaining, or wanting to change the channel. Everyone seems content, at least for a little while, and I have the nicest feeling wash over me—we are at peace.

There are moments from the past that give me "warm fuzzies" when I think about them.

Traveling to Yellowstone in the middle of June when the rain suddenly turns to snow and we stop the car to get out and play. Our fourteen-year-old couldn't remember the white stuff and our nine-year-old had never seen such a sight. That moment was a gift from Above.

On a trip to North Carolina, I listen to our daughters as they work on a latch hook project in the back seat of the van. I like what I hear. The fourteen-year-old is gently helping her younger sister get the hang of it and their talk is easy, natural, and loving.

I look over at my husband who is driving and reach out to pat his shoulder. He turns and smiles. The sun is setting behind the mountains and the last rays filter into the van. I realize that despite all our flaws and imperfections, we are a family bound by love.

I look at my friend with a straight face and tell her the truth, "We are not a perfect family, but we do have some perfect moments."

TOM A. BESSIE

He entered our lives one fall day in 1982. We were never properly introduced, but that didn't seem to matter.

His age was somewhat of a mystery, but his actions were clear—he was mischievous.

"You left your toys out of the sandbox. Go put them away," I said to three-year-old Ginny.

"Tom did it."

"What?" I asked, startled. I didn't know anyone named Tom and I certainly had not seen any young boys in the neighborhood.

"Tom did it. He's always doing naughty things."

"Oh, I see," I answered as the ole' light bulb began to go off in my head. I was no stranger to imaginary friends, having had three of my own when I was younger.

I decided to make a suggestion, "Ginny, why don't you go out and show Tom where all the toys belong so the next time you all play he can help put things away."

She looked up at me with those big, brown eyes and in a serious tone explained, "I can't. Tom went home."

"Well, I guess you're stuck with clean-up duty. Better get moving," I instructed.

Over the next few weeks Tom popped in and out of our lives with a certain regularity. Ginny did nothing wrong; poor Tom did nothing right. It was always Tom who forget to pick up toys, carry dishes off the table and put clothes in the drawer. He was a little stinker.

One day, after Tom's naughty spell, I had a talk with Ginny. I explained that Tom wouldn't be allowed to come over and play again unless he learned some manners. I also told her that since she had such wonderful manners she would be the perfect teacher for Tom.

Her little face formed a frown as she said, "Tom doesn't like manners."

I smiled, "I'm sure he'd love to have good manners like you. Teach him some before he comes over again."

This ploy worked for a while. I had to praise Tom when the room was clean, toys put away, or dishes cleared off the table. The positive reinforcement was getting through to Tom.

Just about the time we had Tom "mannerized," his visits became less frequent. Spring was fast approaching and we were busy outdoors.

When I mentioned Tom's absences to Ginny, she shrugged and said, "He's at home."

We took a vacation to visit grandparents that spring and Ginny never mentioned Tom. She was too busy swimming, playing, and taking walks. It was on one of our walks that my husband mentioned Tom.

Ginny was skipping ahead of us and she turned around and said, "Tom moved."

My husband and I looked at each other and he remarked, "Well, that's a shame. We never even knew his last name."

Ginny stopped skipping, turned to us and announced, "A. Bessie, his full name is Tom A. Bessie and he moved into that house."

As our eyes followed her pointed finger it was all we could do to keep from laughing. She was pointing to a wooden windmill lawn ornament that stood about three feet high.

My husband whispered in my ear, "Not only is Tom A. Bessie invisible, he's real short, too!"

That was the last time Ginny mentioned Tom A. Bessie. She simply outgrew the need for an imaginary friend.

Several years later we happened to be in the same neighborhood and there was the same little windmill lawn ornament.

My husband and I looked at each other and I turned to Ginny in the back seat and asked, "Do you know who lives there?"

She looked out the window and a smile of recognition crossed her face, "Tom A. Bessie."

Good ole' Tom. He may be gone, but he will never be forgotten.

SEARCHING FOR A SWIMSUIT

Looking for a swimsuit is like having a root canal. I don't want to do it, but at times it's necessary.

These past few days I've realized it's an absolute necessity that I get a new one.

My old one died last year. I was sentimentally attached to that suit. I'd had it for years and that was the problem.

One day last August it just snapped—literally. It was not a pretty sight.

Knowing that it takes weeks, sometimes months, to find the right suit, I decided I'd better start my search.

I needed someone to go along to give me an objective opinion.

Several of my friends came to mind, but I decided against asking. They wouldn't want to hurt my feelings.

My husband came to mind next, but he would never do. He's seen me naked so he would not be objective. Besides, he hates to shop and he'd tell me the first one I tried on looked good just to get me out of the store.

I thought of taking my eight-year-old daughter. She's at the age where she thinks I'm the prettiest mommy in the world and I look nice in anything. She would be wonderful for moral support, but not objectivity.

That left my teenage daughter. She's at the age where she's brutally honest. I wanted honesty, not brutality, but I decided on my teenager.

Big mistake.

At the first store she positioned herself outside the dressing room.

As I tried on suit after suit she didn't have to say a word. Her expressions gave me the only answer I needed—rolling eyes, gagging gestures and nods of disapproval.

By the third store I was tired, frustrated and my self-image was at rock bottom.

As I took my usual six-at-a-time items in the dressing room I prayed, "Lord, let me find one suit that looks decent on me, doesn't cost more than a week's groceries and will bring a smile to my daughter's face."

When I opened the dressing room door I realized the Lord has a sense of humor. My teenager looked me over from head to toe and a smile lit up her face. She said, "Are you going to wear THAT in public?"

"No, I plan to wear it in the bathtub!"

I admit my nerves were frayed and hearing the woman in the next stall snickering didn't help matters.

Oh, my teenager was kind in her own way (that brutally honest way). There were some suits that she almost liked on me. She would gently say, "If you just keep your stomach sucked in you'll look fine," or "If you don't put your arms down no one will notice that flab sticking out."

Somehow the image of me walking down the beach holding my arms up in the air seemed a lot worse than my flab sticking out, but then what do I know?

Twenty-six suits and several stores later, I decided to call it quits. I wondered why I brought my teenager along in the first place.

Oh yes, honesty.

I was sick of honesty.

I was ready for a big dose of fantasy.

When we got home I went straight for a catalog, picked out a suit I liked (without asking anyone what they thought), called the company and ordered it.

What if I don't like it when it comes in, or it doesn't look good, or it shows my flab?

No problem—I'll just wear it in the bathtub!

THE REAL DICK and JANE

I know the real Dick and Jane. They have a dog named Sam, not Spot. They are alive and well living in Florida.

The fictional Dick, Jane, and Spot were introduced to me when I began first grade. I loved reading about their adventures even with the limited vocabulary.

From the first introductions over ten years ago, the real Dick and Jane have become part of our extended family. Being a few years older than my husband and me, they have shared their bits of parental wisdom and their sense of humor with us.

Unlike their fictional counterparts, the real Dick and Jane have taken us on some "real" adventures.

We've been canoeing down a body of water called a river that in places was barely wide enough for a single canoe.

The trip should have taken about three hours tops, but we managed to stretch it into seven! There were tipped over canoes, frequent potty stops along the banks, bugs, alligators, and some lousy navigation. We were almost ready to call it quits after that one, but Dick and Jane talked us into a relaxed ride down a natural spring.

The spring was beautiful! The day was hot and sunny and we couldn't wait to hit the water in our inner tubes. However, once my backside met that frigid water, I was ready to get out. The problem was there was no where to go—I was stuck in that big, black, doughnut shaped piece of plastic! When the ride was finally over, my posterior was totally numb.

We decided we'd had enough of water for a while; some road trips might be nice.

We've been over back roads, side roads, winding roads, and roads that didn't deserve to be called roads. It was on one of those back roads that we had our "funniest" adventure yet.

We were out for a nice Sunday drive when Dick decided to take us down a sandy, country road. We were talking when the van hit a big bump; at least we thought it was a big bump. Dick glanced in his rearview mirror and said, "It's moving!"

We all turned to look and we saw the biggest, fattest, snake slowly trying to make its way across the road.

Not being anything remotely close to a snake lover, Dick put the van in reverse and backed over it. We felt the bump, looked out the front and saw the snake moving!

Dick put the van in drive and drove over it again. Another bump. We all turned around and looked at the snake. It did not seem to be moving.

Dick and Scotty decided they would go check to make sure the snake was really dead. They cautiously walked to within three feet of the reptile and Dick yelled to us, "It's a rattler!"

Jane and I watched from the van as they inched their way forward to get a better look.

Jane started laughing and said, "Watch this."

She stuck her head out the window and shouted, "There's another one behind you!"

It's difficult to describe exactly what happened next. I was laughing so much I had tears in my eyes which made it a little hard to focus.

I did see Dick and Scotty jump higher than I've ever seen any men jump before. In mid-air they both managed to do a 180 degree turn to check out their backsides. Their feet barely touched the ground until they were back in the van.

They were not pleased when they saw us rolling on the seats laughing hysterically.

I'm sure if I read this account about the fictional Dick and Jane it would go something like this:

"See Jane shout.

Shout, Jane, shout!

See Dick jump.

Jump, Dick, jump.

See Jane laugh.

Laugh, Jane, laugh.

See Dick run.

Run, Dick, run."

That was one of our more memorable adventures (Jane and I still laugh about it although Dick and Scotty don't find it so amusing).

While the Dick and Jane of my childhood helped me with reading lessons, the Dick and Jane of my adult years have helped me with "life lessons."

I'm glad I know the real Dick and Jane.

FAT CATS CAN JUMP

What is black, tan, and white, weighs twenty pounds and with one leap can land on the kitchen counter? Bandit—the fat cat.

Don't be fooled by her drooping belly and sweet disposition. It's all in her master scheme to throw everyone off guard. She pretends she can do nothing but eat, sleep, and roll over to have her tummy scratched. But beneath that large exterior exists an agility that is amazing.

Bandit's acrobatic skills started surfacing when the vet said it was time to put her on a diet. Diets are no fun for cats, but they're even worse for cat owners.

Foolishly believing that putting Bandit on a diet would be easy (after all, she couldn't open the refrigerator or cabinets and get her own food), I simply put out half a cup of food for her. SCARF! It was gone in thirty seconds and she began meowing for more.

"No, I'm not giving you anymore. That's all the vet said you could have."

The meowing intensified. I stood my ground. I began explaining (to a cat!) why she needed to go on a diet.

"You're just too fat, Bandit. The vet says you'll die soon if you don't lose weight."

I could tell by the look on her face that she didn't care what the vet said. All she cared about was her food.

"Too bad, Bandit. That's it for today," I said as I left to do errands.

When I returned I stopped dead in my tracks in the kitchen. I almost dialed 911. The breakfast dishes in the sink were clean—not a trace of food left on the plates! The last drops of milk had vanished from the glasses.

Who, or what, could have done this?

My first, and only, suspect was Bandit. But she was so fat and lazy she would never exert herself by jumping in the sink—or would she?

"Bandit, did you do this?"

She answered by lazily rolling on her back and meowing for me to scratch her belly.

There was something strange going on ...

A few days later I found a bag of bagels on the kitchen floor. The bag was ripped open and the last onion bagel was missing!

I immediately tracked down Bandit who was sleeping on my younger daughter's bed.

"O.K., let me smell your breath."

Bandit slowly opened one eye and gave me a look that said, "Not on your life."

It didn't matter. I smelled the onions anyway.

I was beginning to worry...

For the next several days the whole family began to notice missing food. Anything left unguarded for more than a minute seemed to mysteriously disappear—peanuts, popcorn, watermelon, chips, and grapes. The cat was not losing any weight. In fact, her sides were beginning to bulge a little more.

The final blow came one afternoon when my older daughter couldn't find her science experiment that consisted of a moldy piece of bread in a plastic baggy.

"Mom, I know I left it on the picnic table, but it's not here."

"Are you sure?"

We looked on the picnic table, but there was no sign of moldy bread. As my daughter looked underneath, she let out a scream, "Bandit!"

The evidence was in the corner—the remains of a plastic baggy with a few scant crumbs.

That night my husband and I discussed the fat cat situation.

"You're just going to have to feed her more."

"I can't. The vet said it would kill her if she's too fat."

"Well, it's killing me the way she eats everything in sight. We won't be able to afford groceries if you keep her on this diet. That cat will eat anything."

"...will eat anything." The phrase kept going through my mind that night which is probably why I had such a terrible dream.

In my dream, Bandit kept getting bigger and bigger. Her appetite kept growing and growing. She started looking at me and licking her lips. I woke up in a cold sweat. That cat was off her diet!

21

I got out of bed and went straight to the kitchen. I got the biggest bowl I could find and poured it full of cat food. I watched as Bandit wolfed it down.

Bandit proved to me that fat cats can jump (when they want to), but hopefully, she'll stay on the ground now where I believe all fat cats belong.

THE COORDINATE MAN AND THE LANDMARK WOMAN

My husband gauges everything by the coordinates north, south, east, and west. I gauge everything by landmarks.

When we're out in the woods, he'll say we're walking due east. I'll say we're walking a little to the left of that tree with the bent limb.

When we're driving, he'll ask if I'm going to turn north or south, and I'll ask if he means left or right. That drives him nuts.

He has no use for landmarks; he's strictly a coordinate man. I have no use for coordinates; I'm strictly a landmark woman. It makes for an interesting marriage—especially on a trip to the mall.

As we pull into a parking space my husband looks over and says, "Remember that we are in the south parking lot."

The girls and I look at each other and then at the closest store—Penney's.

"I'll remember," I assure him.

The girls and I want to browse and shop. My husband, on the other hand, is on a mission. He wants to see every boat displayed for the boat show weekend.

"You go ahead and look and we'll meet you in front of Dillard's in an hour."

"Where's Dillard's?"

We've been coming to the same mall for over ten years, but my husband refuses to learn his way around. This probably has something to do with the fact that he only goes "malling" once or twice a year. It is not his favorite past time.

"Remember the Dollar Store? Dillard's is right beside the Dollar Store."

"How far down?"

"It's not too far. You turn by the fountain."

"Do I turn north or south? What fountain?"

I give him one of those looks. "You turn left from here. You decide if it's north or south. The fountain is that big cement pond looking thing in the middle of the mall. If you can't find it, just ask someone."

I KNOW my husband will not ask for directions. He'll keep going and going until he eventually finds where he needs to be or decides he didn't need to be there in the first place. It all depends on his tolerance level for that day.

The hour passes quickly. The girls and I head toward Dillard's and we meet my husband coming the other way.

"Why didn't you wait for us at Dillard's?"

"There's just too many people. I figured you'd be coming this way."

"Well, your homing instincts were right."

We walk a few more steps and I stop and put my hand on my husband's arm.

"Honey, did you even go to Dillard's?"

He looks me square in the eye. "No—what difference does that make?"

"Oh, none," I say with a smile, "but I just can't understand how a man who can find his way around the woods can get lost in a mall."

He turns and glares, "Well, I don't understand how a woman who can find her way around this jungle of stores can't tell north from south!"

Our teenager, who has been listening to this conversation and who has been on camping trips with her dad, leans over and whispers, "Daddy doesn't really know where he is all the time in the woods. I think he carries one of those clappers in his truck so he can find his way around."

Even though I knew she was teasing (at least I think she was teasing), it was enough to make me go into a fit of laughter.

"What's so funny?" my husbands asks suspiciously.

"I'll tell you in the van."

"By the way, how do we get out of here?"

The girls and I look at each other and together we say, "Through Penney's!"

As we fasten our seat belts in the parking lot outside Penney's, a thought crosses my mind: Between the coordinate man, the landmark woman, and their two daughters, will the tan van *ever* find its way home?

A GOODNIGHT KISS

We had not talked for years, Elva and I. What had once been a close friendship dwindled to an annual Christmas card and letter. It was no one's fault really—time and distance took their toll. We did manage to keep in touch somewhat by mutual friends. It was through a mutual friend that I learned of the recent tragedy.

A long distance call in the afternoon is either very good news or very bad news. In this case it was the latter.

My friend, Sue, from Virginia called to tell me that Elva's seventeen-year-old son, Dustin, had been killed in a car accident. In a car that Elva and her husband bought for him. On a stretch of curving, mountainous road that seemed to claim a young life almost annually.

The first thought was disbelief. I went to the photo album and took out the latest Christmas card photo of Elva and her family. There was Dustin. A young man now, tall, handsome, smiling for the camera. Dead? Not possible.

I thought back to the times my husband and I baby-sat for Dustin and his younger sister. He was only four at the time, but what a dynamo; always busy, always questioning, always into everything, and always looking up at me with those big, saucer shaped blue eyes.

I also remembered a school-aged Dustin. All arms and legs, much more reserved, but always the twinkle in those blue eyes.

Through the years Elva kept me up to date on the children's lives. Dustin going to the state track meet, Dustin being so involved in church activities, and Dustin taking college courses his senior year. This promising young life was now over?

That night I told my older daughter about Dustin. She didn't remember him that well, but she did remember the photos and stories. She looked thoughtful for a moment, turned to her friend who was spending the night (and who happened to have a seventeen-year-old brother at home) and said, "Just think how quiet it would be at your house without your brother."

Ah yes, the quiet. How will Elva cope with the quiet times? The times when she listens for Dustin's voice only to remember she won't hear it, the times she'll walk by his room only to remember she won't see him, and the times she'll think of something to tell him only to remember he's not there.

I can't begin to imagine the pain of losing a child. I don't want to even try. It just doesn't seem to be the Right Order of Life (if one existed).

Parents are supposed to die before their children, not the other way around.

After saying special prayers for Elva and her family that night, I said an extra prayer of thanks for my own family. My family that was all under one roof, all healthy and safe, at least for now. A tragedy reminds us how vulnerable we all are—nothing should be taken for granted.

I quietly got out of bed and went into my younger daughter's room. I watched her sleeping with one arm hanging over the bed and her hair covering her face. I gently pushed the hair back, rolled her over, kissed her goodnight again, and whispered "I love you" in her ear. She didn't respond. Mr. Sandman had already claimed her.

I walked into my older daughter's room. She and her friend were still awake, whispering. I went over and kissed her on the forehead.

"You already kissed me goodnight. Why are you kissing me again?"

"Because I love you."

And because a mother never knows when a goodnight kiss will have to last a lifetime.

COUNTRY MUSIC CONVERTS

The whole mess started with Mike Giles and a trip to Nags Head.

My husband and I shared the same taste in music up until that trip to the Outer Banks with friends.

We were musically in sync as we sang along with the same kind of songs. We had nightly quizzes with our daughters, "Name That Oldie Tune," to make them appreciate our music.

Our teenage daughter was not thrilled with the quiz game and there were times when my husband would say, "Quick— what group did this song?"

She would stare blankly and then say, "I don't know."

In reality this meant "I don't care," but the point is she did say something and we did eventually get her to recognize the great CCR songs.

Our younger daughter, being more impressionable and easier to mold, could always be counted on to know the Beach Boys.

So there we sat, every evening around the dinner table, the four of us eating and listening (or pretending to listen) to good ole' rock n' roll music. It was a scene befitting a Norman Rockwell painting.

Then came that fateful Thanksgiving vacation.

After being on the road for almost fifteen hours we were overjoyed to find the beach house on our third try. As we wearily got out of the van, a strange noise broke the silence. It sounded almost like a wail.

We looked at each other and decided this might not be our house after all.

Suddenly the doors flew open and our friends came out followed by the sounds of COUNTRY MUSIC!

We didn't know what to say. Had they been possessed? Were they deaf? Was this the only station they could get? If so, turn it OFF!

My first question was WHY? Why were they listening to this stuff?

Mike informed us that he was now a country music fan and his wife, Janet, had been converted as well! We were all shaken up by this revelation. Here was Mike, a good college buddy who loved rock n' roll, now crossing the line to country music. It was enough to make us want to turn around and go back home.

We did stay and we had a wonderful vacation with the exception of those moments we were subjected to country music.

On the way home we discussed our friends' new-found musical tastes. The girls and I agreed they were crazy to listen to that stuff. My husband was strangely silent and then he spoke up, "Well, it really isn't too bad once you get used to it."

The girls and I stared at him as if he had three heads, but he just kept on driving and we kept on listening to good ole' rock n' roll.

A few weeks later, I walked into my husband's workshop and was shocked to hear the strains of a country music song coming from his radio.

I was worried.

"Are you going through some kind of mid-life crisis?"

"No, I just like to listen to it sometimes."

Soon he was listening not only in the workshop, but also in his truck as well. He would get nasty if anyone tried to change the station. We were all worried.

It wasn't long before our younger daughter came bounding in the house one day singing a country song! She was beginning to have that trademark whine in her voice.

"Just where did you hear that young lady?" I snapped.

"Out in the building with Daddy," she answered as she skipped past me.

This country music business was getting out of hand.

I walked into my older daughter's room only to find her listening to a country station! When she saw me she quickly flipped to another station.

"I was just... flipping through," she stammered.

"Good thing," I muttered.

I was soon outnumbered. The three of them were being converted before my very eyes. I was the outsider. I felt alone at dinner as they discussed country music songs and artists. I longed for the old days when we listened to decent music.

♥ KWITCHYERBELLYAKIN ♥

The final blow came when we decided to go on vacation.

Our older daughter taped FOUR hours of nonstop country music to listen to on her headphones, but my family chose to play that tape so everyone could hear (against my protests).

I was subjected to twelve hours of country music. My family sang along. They laughed. They played the same songs over and over. I tried to use my daughter's headphones, but I couldn't drown out the sound.

What I did next changed our family—I gave up. I listened. Maybe it wasn't too bad.

By the time we returned home, I knew the words to most of the songs. I even sang along with a couple of them.

So now we sit around the dinner table, the four of us, eating and listening to country music. The scene hasn't changed — just the music.

TEENAGE TRANSLATIONS

There is a picture on our wall collage of my older daughter hugging my leg. She is twenty-two months old and about thigh high. The look on her face is one of territorial happiness. She seems to be saying, "This is MY mommy and I love her."

My daughter is a teenager now. She hasn't hugged my thigh in years and she is only territorial about her room, yet I know she still loves me.

How do I know this? Because I used to be where she is now.

The teenage years are hard for parents and children alike. Children want to grow up and parents want to keep them small for as long as possible.

I think it's up to parents to remember what being a teenager is like and to interpret what they're really saying to us.

When I signed up to volunteer at my daughter's Junior High she told me in a very diplomatic way that she knew I was busy, and since I'd volunteered all those years in elementary school, I really didn't have to in Junior High.

Teenage Translation: "Mom, please don't come within ten feet of my new school. Only come on Parent's Night and to pick me up when I'm sick. Please don't ever do anything to embarrass me like putting your finger in your mouth and then wiping off my face."

Mother Translation: "I am never too busy to be involved with your education. The school needs volunteers. You need me, you just don't realize it now."

Things got more interesting as my daughter got more involved in activities. Moms in car pools were looked on as taxi drivers.

"Mom, just blow the horn and they'll come out."

Teenage Translation: "Don't make me walk to the door to get them. No one does that anymore."

Mother Translation: "The horn is used for emergencies. You will use the manners you've been taught and walk to that door."

She walks, but not without giving me one of those I-can't-believe-you're-making-me-do-this looks.

In the ten seconds it takes her to walk back to the car she has already apologized to her friend for my "old fashioned ways."

The phone stage is every parent's nightmare. I never knew my daughter had so many friends until they all started calling at dinner. We have an iron clad rule in our home that no one answers the phone during dinner.

Teenage Translation: "I can't believe they won't let me answer the phone. I haven't talked to Chrissy for at least forty-five minutes. Something probably happened and I won't know about it until they let me away from this table. Who needs to eat? I need to talk on the phone!"

Mother Translation: "It's amazing that she can sit through dinner and barely say two words, but put that phone up to her ear and she talks nonstop!"

There are other times when a simple disagreement leads to a nasty argument. Her temper flares, her eyes roll, and I am given the look of teenage disgust.

It makes my blood boil. Something in those eyes—the look, the defiance, it takes me back twenty-five years and I am the one looking out at my own mother.

Teenage Translation: "I can't believe you treat me like a child. I can make my own decisions! You just don't trust me!"

Mother Translation: "I can't believe you're so grown-up. I still see you as six years old and needing to hold my hand. It's not you I don't trust, it's the world. I don't want you to get hurt. I love you."

I realize that my role in my daughter's life is changing. She has gone from hugging my thigh to quickly kissing my cheek. She is growing up.

I know I'm still a player in my daughter's life, maybe not the central one all the time, but I fit in. Sometimes I'm in the background, sometimes in the foreground, but I'm always in the picture, somewhere, trying to interpret what she is really saying to me.

THE ADDRESS BOOK OF LIFE

The red pen made a diagonal slash through the name and address in my book. This one hurt. No one died, but a relationship did.

This family no longer existed as it had before with a mom, a dad, and their two children living in the same house. They were split up now—divorced—with the children shuffling back and forth between the parents. Their marriage lasted many years, and to outsiders looking in, it seemed a near perfect union. They prayed together, played together, and stayed together until one day the wife decided she needed space. This space did not include her husband and children.

She left behind a devastated husband, bewildered children, shocked friends, and a lifestyle most would envy.

WHY?

No one really knows and probably never will.

What possesses some people to just up and walk out on a relationship after twenty years? What went so wrong that it could not be fixed?

I don't know, but I do know what comes after the divorce: pain and suffering, doubt, and mistrust of emotions.

It hurts to see good friends go through something like this. It hurts to put that red mark through what used to be a "happy family."

The disturbing fact is that isn't the only red mark I have in my address book—it is only the latest. I sift through the pages and each red mark puts a little stab of fear in my heart.

These marriages all started out like my own—two people in love vowing to commit to each other for the rest of their lives. But somewhere, somehow, that commitment was broken.

I realize that for some people, divorce is the only answer to save their sanity or their life. I can understand their need to sever that kind of relationship.

What I don't understand is the relative ease with which most people these days end a commitment. What about the relationship that dies due to lack of interest? Or the marriage that fails because it would take too much "work" to put it back together?

Marriage, it seems to me, is like riding a roller coaster. There are highs and lows and some shaky turns along the way, but it's important to hang on till the ride is over.

Divorce is stopping halfway up the incline.

I hope when friends put my name down beside my husband's in their address books, it stays. If there does have to be a mark put through it at some point, I hope it will be because one of us died—not our marriage.

I'm hoping to ride this roller coaster till it stops.

MEMORY KEEPERS

The young girl is looking over her shoulder as if she's about to say something. Her dark hair is swinging around her chin. She's caught in mid-step as she's walking down a narrow dirt road. There is a large, white house on the left in front of her.

I stare at the picture in my hands. I wish I knew what the young girl was going to say. I wish I knew exactly how old she is in the picture. I wish someone had written all that information on the back.

That young girl is my mother. My mother, who never liked to have her picture taken, died at the age of forty-seven.

Of course, I remember what my mother looked like, but my two daughters are curious. They ask questions. What did Mimmie look like? When did she start wearing glasses? Do I look like her? Did she have freckles?

I wish I could point to a portrait or whip out some nice, clear pictures, but there are none. The pictures I do have are very old and she is very young in them (not the way I remember her).

The few that were taken in her last years are blurry or she has her hand up to her face. There is no way my daughters can see her warm, brown eyes, the faint freckles across her nose, and the way her lips turned into a quick smile with a little dimple on her right cheek.

They have to rely on me to tell them these important things and I do, but it would be so much easier and nicer if I had some pictures to back up the descriptions.

"See Mimmie's salt and pepper hair? Well, she always had trouble with graying early. Look at all those freckles on her arms. See those bangs? Now you girls know where we get those little bangs that drive us crazy."

I cringe at the thought of the only clear picture I have of my mother—her driver's license! In it she looks like a candidate for "America's Most Wanted." It is ironic that the only clear picture is the one that bears the least resemblance.

I decided after my husband and I got married that lack of pictures would not be a problem in our home. I have kept my word.

I may have gone slightly overboard according to my family. My husband wishes he had bought stock in Kodak before I went on my "mission." My daughters have nicknamed me "Debbie Kodak." My cousin insists that a telephoto lens is going to start growing from my eye any day.

Their taunts don't deter me. I plunge ahead with my "aim, click, develop" routine.

It is a routine that has resulted in thousands of pictures, none of which I can bear to part with. Sure, some are a little out of focus (I can still tell it's my younger daughter's blurred face as she's toddling toward me). Some show only a hand (but I know it's my older daughter telling me to wait till she gets her hair fixed). Some show a sideways view of our kitchen as I snapped too soon when I put the film in the camera.

There are others, though, that are truly priceless. My older daughter at eighteen months standing by a pickle barrel with her thumb in her mouth looking so content. My younger daughter at three months smiling at my husband.

One of my favorite pictures is my husband holding a Wahoo with the biggest grin on his face while his boat is sinking in the background (his smile changed when he turned to see his boat sinking by the dock, but I have the happy moment on film).

Another prized photo is my younger daughter with the biggest fat lip I've ever seen. Her swollen lip was the result of a careless turn on her bike. She is crying in the picture, but moments after the "click" of the camera her tears turned to laughter as I promised her a milkshake. All the information is written on the back of the picture in case anyone forgets that eventful evening.

My all-time favorite picture of my older daughter is one that I promised I'd never show anyone (but I never promised that I wouldn't talk about it). She is almost four years old and we had just returned from a day at the beach. She is sitting on the toilet, naked, looking at a book. Her little body is so tan it almost looks as if she still has on her swimsuit. Her dark, curly hair is falling around her face and as I call her name she turns to look at me. Those large brown eyes are questioning, "Yes, Mommy?" Looking at that picture is remembering a wonderful day at the beach with my family.

My one special memory keeper is a picture that was taken of my husband and me on our wedding day. It is not a posed picture. It was taken as we walked out the church door when we thought we were alone. We were laughing and my husband turned and gave me the biggest kiss. We were married! Seeing that picture in our wedding album reminds me of one of the happiest days of my life.

To me, that's the whole purpose of pictures—they are memory keepers. They show a brief moment in life that somehow gives way to more memories until that day, or that party, or that event, becomes so clear it's like living it all over again.

My children, future grandchildren, and future great-grandchildren will never have to wonder about the pictures they inherit. All the information is written on the back. They won't have to second guess their memory keepers.

They might, however, wonder about that telephoto lens growing out of my eye!

A HAMSTER, A CAT, AND A LESSON IN LIFE

"The cat killed the hamster."

"Oh no!" I stared at my husband in disbelief. I could feel the tears starting to roll down my cheeks. Not so much for the dear departed Cinnamon, but for our eight-year-old daughter, Megan, who thought the world of her hamster.

My first reaction, I'm ashamed to say, was to suggest that maybe we could get her another one and she wouldn't notice the difference.

"How do you propose we do that?" asked my husband.

"Well, I remember when I was a little girl my canary died and my mother didn't want to tell me. She told me Santa Claus had to come early that year to get my sick canary and that he would bring him back at Christmas—and he did."

My husband just stared at me. "Do you think she'll go for that?"

"No, not really. But how do you think she's going to feel when she finds out that Bandit killed Cinnamon?"

Now it was my husband's turn to make an off-the-wall suggestion. "We could put him back in the cage and pretend he just died during the night."

We both looked at each other. No, that wouldn't work. The only thing left was the truth.

A few minutes later Megan came out of her room all teary-eyed and sobbing as she said, "Cinnamon got out of his cage and I can't find him!"

Most mothers in that situation would have hugged their daughter and gently told her the truth. Not me. Oh, I hugged her, but when I looked into those big, wet eyes there was no way I was going to tell her. Thinking about how much she loved that little rodent broke my heart. She needed the truth, but I couldn't give it to her. I did the next best thing. I whispered, "You need to go tell Daddy."

As Megan wandered into the bedroom to find her daddy, I felt something akin to what a mother lion must feel when she senses danger to her cub. I wanted to yell "Please don't tell her!" (we could just pretend that Cinnamon ran away from home never to be found again), while another part of me wanted to yell, "Please tell her-QUICK!"

My husband told her in a nice, gentle, daddy kind of way. He told her about a cat's instincts and how Bandit was just doing what came naturally to her, told her about the time his brother's dog killed his rabbit, told her that Cinnamon had gotten out of his cage and Bandit was just protecting her territory.

After that explanation was it any easier to accept that one animal she loved killed another animal she loved?

I watched her as she dried her face and walked slowly toward her room. I saw her step on Bandit's paw—just hard enough to make Bandit jump and run for cover. It was a hard truth to accept.

That evening we had graveside services for Cinnamon. We buried him beside the fish and the iguana at the edge of our yard. My husband made a small cross for the recently departed and we said prayers over the grave as Cinnamon made his way to Hamster Heaven.

The things we go through to save our children from pain—the pain of life of which death is certainly a part.

We want to shield them, protect them, and comfort them because when they hurt, we as parents hurt twice as much. We fail to remember that out of that pain usually comes growth and strength and understanding plus an ability to cope with other life tragedies. We also fail to remember how resilient children are.

A prime example of this is Megan's acceptance of her new hamster. He looks like Cinnamon, only smaller. His name is Pepper.

We're hoping to keep Bandit from ever meeting our newest addition.

FALLing MEMORIES

My children will never experience fall in Florida. This fact was made painfully clear to me the other day when my older daughter remarked, "This is great football weather!"

Her younger sister agreed and added, "That's because it's fall now."

WHAT?! The temperature is in the eighties, the air conditioner is running full blast, my hair has flopped from the humidity, and I may even be having a premature hot flash! This is not my idea of fall weather.

Fall is waking up in a room that's just a bit chilly and pulling an extra blanket over you while you catch another ten minutes of shut-eye. It's walking outside to feel the nip in the air and seeing Jack Frost's handiwork on the lawn. Fall is walking in the woods on a crisp, clear day and watching your breath come out in soft puffs as the leaves crunch beneath your feet.   Fall is shedding your sweater at noon because it's much too warm outside and then putting it on again at sundown because it's much too cool.   It's a brisk walk in the early evening when you smell smoke coming from the neighboring chimneys, hear the steady raking of leaves in someone's yard, and smell the wonderful aroma of homemade soup simmering on the stove as you walk in the back door.

Yes, fall is football weather, but it's the kind where everyone brings a blanket, a thermos of hot chocolate, and a good set of lungs to yell for the team.

It's listening to the bands play at half-time, watching the cheerleaders, and ordering hot dogs with chili from the concession stand.

As much as my heart longs to be back to see the glory and splendor those old mountains put on this month a part of me understands what will come next—WINTER. I do not miss winter.

I take another look at my children, now outdoors and enjoying the "cool" weather, and I realize that as they grow up their perception of fall will be much different from mine. That's fine as long as they can look back on this time of year and like what they remember.   For I believe you keep your good memories and leave the others behind.

Fall in the mountains is one memory definitely worth keeping.

THE MOMMY GENE

A woman gains more than just weight during pregnancy; she gains a new gene. I call it the "Mommy Gene," and although medical science doesn't acknowledge its existence, I have no doubt every mother has been blessed with one.

I believe the gene is a trade-off for all the brain cells a woman loses during birth. I know everyone won't agree with this, but let me present some evidence (personal, not scientific).

Before I became a mother I was organized. My desk at work was uncluttered, I could finish a sentence without pausing to remember what the heck I was talking about, I could remember the names of people I just met, I could go to the grocery store without a list, and I even managed to walk out of the house every morning alert and ready for a new day.

Fast forward now to a few weeks after the birth of my first daughter. I no longer had a desk at work, the house was a disaster, I only spoke in syllables, I could barely remember my own name, I never went to the grocery store, and when I did venture outside, my appearance made small children run for cover.

That first Christmas of motherhood I did manage to address all my Christmas cards. I was so proud! Getting all those cards in the mail was quite an accomplishment for me considering my disorganized lifestyle.

Imagine my surprise when the sympathetic postman brought them all back to me. I had forgotten to put stamps on eighty-five cards!

I felt I was losing more than a few brain cells that day as I raced up the steps to the post office with my infant daughter in one arm and the unstamped Christmas cards in the other.

The line was VERY long and I was VERY tired by the time I finally got to the counter.

"I need eighty-five stamps," I said breathlessly as I reached in my purse and threw some bills on the counter (at least I thought they were bills).

The postal clerk cleared his throat and asked, "Is this how you want to pay for your stamps?"

Everyone behind me fell silent. My daughter's snowsuit hood was covering my face and as I shifted her to my other arm I saw what I had thrown on the counter. So did everyone else.

For what seemed like hours, but in reality was only a matter of seconds, no one moved, no one said anything. Everyone just looked at the counter and then back at me.

I wanted to say, "What's the matter—no one ever tried to pay for stamps with *nursing pads* before?" But the only thing I could manage was a soft, "Oh my."

The clerk was still staring at the pads as if I had put some slithering reptile in front of him.

I grabbed the nursing pads (unused, thank goodness!), stuck them in my purse, mumbled that I would get the stamps another day, and practically ran out of the building.

I vowed I would never ever step foot in that post office again. But I did and I owe it all to the Mommy Gene. It's that little bit of genetic material that keeps all mothers running in spite of pain, humiliation, and lack of sleep.

It's the Mommy Gene that makes our eyes fly open at 2 a.m. when we hear the words, "Mommy, I feel sick."

It's the Mommy Gene that makes those of us who can't stand the sight of blood hold our child's hand and whisper, "It will be all right" as our child's bloody face is being stitched.

It's the Mommy Gene that makes a mother stay well while the rest of her family is throwing up in every available toilet and sink.

It's the Mommy Gene that makes a mother forget all the naughty things her child did or said that day and simply smile as she watches her child sleep.

The trade off between the brain cells and the Mommy Gene is quite simple: we lose some things that aren't that important (who really needs short term memory?!), but we gain something priceless—motherhood.

It's been a fair deal for me.

A LAST WALK WITH IDA

The mud oozed around my ankles and covered the top of my borrowed boots with every step. It was difficult to walk up the hill after the recent rain. It was even more difficult to walk up the hill behind a casket.

Simply putting one foot in front of the other and moving forward was a concentrated effort. The narrow, dirt road leading to the family cemetery was in such bad shape that the hearse could not make the first incline, so the pall bearers were struggling and sliding under the weight of the casket.

I found myself wondering how much the casket weighed. I knew it must be a lot because six men were grappling with it and any one of them could have picked up Ida under one arm and walked the distance.

Ida, my dear, sweet aunt who was almost like a grandmother to me, was in that casket. It was hard to believe.

Just a hair above five feet and weighing less than ninety pounds, Ida seemed more child-like than grown-up. Her face was free from the deep wrinkles that seem to come with age. Only small, fine lines etched her mouth—expression lines as she called them. Her blue eyes sparkled with life and zest as much at seventy-six as they did when she was a young woman. Only her snow white hair gave any indication of her true age and everyone seemed to overlook that once they met her.

To know Ida was to know an innocence that doesn't seem to exist anymore. It was to know someone who was *truly* good.

Ida was my mother's oldest sister and matriarch of a family that was left without both parents at a young age. She had a special way with children and could always calm even the fussiest baby.

Ida never married and she never had any children (at least in childbirth), yet she was a "mother" to more children than I can imagine. She had over fifteen nieces and nephews, and at different times in her life she took care of all of us.

One of the special treats that Ida gave her nieces and nephews was taking us for walks in the woods. We loved running along in the woods, hiking up and down different trails, wading in the creeks, and playing on the "Witch Rock". The Witch Rock was a huge boulder (at least that's the way it looked to me) with a crack in the middle. Ida would often tell us stories of people who tried to go through that crack, but for one reason or another never made it. I think she told that story for the benefit of some of my more adventuresome cousins who wanted to try their hand at passing through the rock.

We always took a picnic lunch with us and while we ate Ida would tell us more stories. Sometimes she'd tell us fairy tales and sometimes she'd tell us about the grandparents none of us really knew. She'd talk about her childhood and about how our parents acted when they were younger. We loved those stories, especially since our parents weren't around to disagree.

Ida was never too busy to pretend with us. When we were with her we became princesses, pirates, knights, ghosts, or treasure hunters. She always played along.

We didn't realize it in our childhood, but Ida gave us our heart's desire. She accepted us for what we were, she praised us for each accomplishment, and she loved us all unconditionally.

It was hard to think of that spirit and spunk now being confined to the casket going slowly up the hill.

When we made it to Ida's final resting place, my cousin leaned over and whispered to me, "I'm so glad we had all those walks in the woods with Ida. I'm just sorry this is the last one."

So am I...so am I.

A LESSON LEARNED IN SILENCE

"Don't forget to feed the rabbits after you do the dishes," I croaked to my older daughter.

"Gee, Mom, it was kinda nice when you couldn't talk."

"What?!"

"Well, no offense or anything, but it was nice when you didn't keep reminding us what we needed to do all the time."

Hmm....Keep reminding us what to do.

Of course I remind my daughters what to do—that's part of my duty as a mother, part of my job description. I need to remind my children what to do. What would happen if I didn't?

The answer was a shock. It *would* get done. Oh, maybe not by my standards or by my timetable, but it would get done. My daughters proved it to me just last week.

I had a bad case of laryngitis and I simply could not speak above a whisper. I felt lousy so I didn't bother with my usual verbal reminders.

Thinking back the week had been a nice one. There was no arguing, no bickering, no one complaining about their chores. The rabbits didn't starve, the cat didn't die from malnutrition, and the hamster was still running merrily on his wheel.

Their rooms weren't spotless, but they were livable. The dishes weren't cleaned directly after dinner, but they were finished before bedtime.

The conversations at the dinner table had been pleasant all week and that started me thinking: Was I a better mother when I kept my mouth shut? What a terrible thought!

As my voice grew stronger the next week, my verbal reminders grew weaker. I began to listen more and what I heard was surprising.

The girls didn't argue as much as I remembered. They actually resolved their differences without me. There was none of the familiar, "I'm telling Mom!"

Homework was finished and lunches were packed without reminders from me. Suddenly, they seemed so independent.

Maybe I should feign laryngitis about once a month to keep them in line or maybe I should just weigh my words very carefully before I speak.

THE SHOPPING TRIP

"Would it be OK if we meet you back here in an hour?"

Her question caught me off guard. I was not expecting it. I looked into the face of my 12-going-on-18-year-old daughter.

In the ten seconds it took me to answer some milestones of her young life flashed before me: The first time I let her walk to a friend's house. (I stood in the yard and watched the whole time.) The first night she went to a sleep over. (I called twice to check on her.) The first day she rode her bike to school. (I followed at a safe distance.) And now she wanted to walk through the mall without me?!

She and a friend wanted to wander aimlessly from store to store without an adult present who could dispense wisdom about their choice of clothes.

I eyed them both carefully. I started to give my "don't-talk-to-strangers" lecture, decided against it, then went with my original intent.

"OK, you may go. Remember, don't talk to any strangers, hang on to your purse, make sure you really like something before you buy it, don't spend all your money in one place..."

I realized I was rambling by the impatient looks on their faces. I gave a final nod of approval and they were off.

Watching my daughter and her friend walk away was a milestone in my life.

How many times had I longed for the day when I could go to the mall by myself?

Now I had to resist the urge to run after them.

Wild thoughts were quickly filling my mind. What if someone stole their money? What if someone tried to kidnap them? What if they forgot to come back on time?

I walked into the nearest store, hoping that no one could tell by looking at me how panicky I was feeling. A display of baby cards caught my attention. It didn't seem so long ago that my daughter was a baby herself. It seemed like yesterday that I was pushing her in the stroller from store to store just looking, and now she was looking without me. It wasn't pity that I was feeling rather than the swiftness of passing time.

When did she get so big? How could she be this old when I remembered her so young? How many things did I fail to teach her?

I wandered from store to store not really concentrating on anything until it was time to meet my daughter and her friend. I saw them long before they saw me. They were a sight for anxious eyes.

"Oh Mom, look what we bought."

They excitedly showed me their purchases. I complimented them on their shopping ability and suggested we head home.

Listening to them as we walked to the car I felt foolish for having had such crazy thoughts about a little shopping trip. Yes, this was such a successful outing that I think we'll do it again—when she's 25!

A CRYBABY PUSHING FORTY

"Turn on the water works, Paula Kay!"

That was my daddy's favorite expression when I started to cry. It made no difference that my name was not Paula Kay. I knew what he meant—I was being a crybaby.

It was a well-known fact that Paula Kay, one of my older cousins, was the Queen of Crybabies. I was following a little too closely in her footsteps.

Paula Kay eventually outgrew her crybaby reign, but she passed the crown to me. Unfortunately, that crown still fits.

I know I am not the only adult who tears up easily, but I am one of the few who can admit it.

Tempa, a dear friend, is another self-proclaimed crybaby. She let me know, soon after we met, that she could cry at supermarket openings. I was thrilled. In Tempa I found a kindred spirit.

We understand each other. We realize that we are showing our emotions to the world. We are wearing our hearts on our sleeves.

It is not easy being a crybaby in a world where crying is viewed as childish and immature. It is not easy to be viewed as emotional, not having enough control to wait until the sanctuary of home to shed those tears.

Being a crybaby is part of me and I can no more rid myself of it than I can my freckles.

What I didn't realize, until recently, was that living in a near-state-of-tears-depending-on-my-mood was not such a terrible thing. So what if I am the only one who tears up at a phone commercial picturing a sweet baby? Or cries every time I watch a sad movie? Or chokes up when a sad, country song is played? Or waves as my daughters go off to school each fall with a lump in my throat and tears in my eyes?

My younger daughter once gave me a very special birthday gift, a story she had written just for me. She had worked on this story for a long time alone in her room with the door closed. I had no idea what she was "making" me for my big day.

When my birthday arrived and she proudly presented me with her present, I cried. I cried because I was happy that she took so much time to write the story for me.

I cried because I was touched that she was learning that giving from the heart is the best present of all.

She did not understand my tears at first.

"Don't you like it, Mommy?" she asked with questioning eyes.

"I love it!" I said as I choked back more tears.

I hope a gift from the heart will always bring a tear to my eye.

♥ KWITCHYERBELLYAKIN ♥

I hope I never stop being touched by the little things in life.

I hope in twenty years I can write another story called, "A Crybaby Pushing Sixty."

There are worse things in life I could be.

PANTYHOSE PHOBIA

We women are decision makers. We make important decisions everyday concerning our family and our work.

There is one decision, however, that will bring us to our knees. What kind of pantyhose do we buy? We refer to this as "Pantyhose Phobia," the fear of making a rational decision about the size or color of pantyhose. It is a dilemma that is faced by all women regardless of age or weight.

We all know about the pantyhose section of the store. It is an area we avoid and only venture into in case of an emergency. It is that section where we see lost souls milling about looking dazed and confused. Young children fall asleep in the carts unable to stay awake for Mom's decision. We feel the panic in the air as we pass and we hope that no one asks us for our opinion. For if we are stopped then we, too, are sucked into that vacuum of indecision.

Most women have had bad experiences with pantyhose; perhaps that is why we dislike shopping for them so much. At one time or another we have all made the wrong choice about size—coming home with pantyhose that wouldn't fit an eighteen inch doll and no amount of tugging would budge them past our calves. If we didn't buy them too small, then we picked a "roomy" size where the nylon fit snugly under our arms. As we struggled to roll the excess down it gave new meaning to the word "waistband."

Color is almost as bad. One brand's white is another brand's cream. We have all been guilty of buying more than one pair of pantyhose to make sure we got the "right" color.

Think about it...we can't try pantyhose on in the store, we can't open the package, we have to guess at the size and we look at the color through plastic! Is it any wonder it puts fear into our hearts?

There are rare occasions when we find the perfect fit and color. Wonderful! We rush back to the same store to buy more, only to be told that particular size or style is discontinued.

In the interest of fairness there is one advantage of Pantyhose Phobia—female bonding. There is no other place like the pantyhose section, where women ask complete strangers their opinions, where horror stories about bad fits are shared and where there is a chance friendships may develop.

One Saturday afternoon I decided that I could no longer put off buying pantyhose. I HAD to go. I told my husband I would be back in a few minutes. When I returned home over an hour later, my husband was almost frantic.

"Where have you been? I've been worried sick," he said.

Before I could answer my older daughter looked at me and said, "I told Daddy not to worry, that you were just looking at pantyhose. I told him you always take so long because you talk to all those women."

"I just needed to decide which pair of pantyhose to buy."

"It took an hour and a half for that?!"

"No, it only took me about fifteen minutes once Pat and Linda helped me."

"Pat and Linda? Who are they?"

"Oh, they're the nicest women! Pat noticed that I was having trouble deciding which size to get because I was holding up a pair of both A and B sizes, you know sometimes I'm right in the middle of A and B. Anyway, Pat came over and told me that brand runs large so I should go with the A. Then Linda helped me with the color. I was going to go with the Misty Black, but she suggested the Off Black."

"Well, what did you do the rest of the time?"

"I helped Pat and Linda. I couldn't leave them there alone after they were so kind to me.

"Pat was having trouble deciding between light support and regular support. She said she was up and down quite a bit at her job, (she works at a local junior high), so Linda and I suggested the light support. Of course, then we had to decide on colors. It's important to have everything match.

"We also needed to help Linda. She was trying to decide between a reinforced toe or a sandalfoot. See, with a reinforced toe you don't get holes as easily, but it doesn't look as good with open-toed shoes, so it's a real problem. Pat and I just told her to get both."

My husband looked at me with a confused expression as he said, "I just can"t believe you sometimes."

"Listen, it's no piece of cake trying to buy something for your legs that fits, feels good and looks good at the same time. I'll take all the help I can get."

The next morning I put on the new pantyhose. Ah, great fit! Pat and Linda advised me well.

As I reached down to put on my shoe, my bracelet snagged my hose. A run! A big run creeping up my leg! The dress was definitely out for today.

My husband suggested I wear pants. Good idea! Just as I reached for the pants, Pantyhose Phobia came over me. I'd have to wear knee high hose with the pants! I opened my hose drawer and stared at the tangled mess of knee highs.

Decisions, decisions...now where were Pat and Linda when I needed them?

A BIRTHDAY SURPRISE

It was hard to keep a secret for almost a year, but since a fortieth birthday surprise was involved, I managed.

My husband, Scotty, was adamant about no surprise party or any kind of party for his big 4-0. Being the loyal, trustworthy wife that I am, I agreed. However, I did not agree to NO surprises—just no parties.

Little did he know that I had been plotting for months with our good friends in Virginia, Dennis and Sue. We had decided they would fly down a few days before Scotty's birthday to give him a big surprise.

As the date drew nearer, I found it was harder than I imagined to keep the secret from him. Having been together for so long he knows me quite well and he can usually tell when I'm up to something. My laughter is inappropriate, I twitch around the mouth, and my speech is much too fast. Of course,

I act like that on normal days, too. It's just more pronounced when I'm trying to keep a secret.

The week before Dennis and Sue arrived I found myself biting my tongue—a lot! I would start to say things such as, "Oh, I just can't wait till..." and then I'd catch myself and try to make amends which usually made it worse.

"Wait till what?"

"Oh, I just can't wait till we clean out the garage." Then I'd proceed to giggle, have several twitches around the mouth, and talk nonstop for the next several minutes.

He gave me lots of strange looks.

I got to the point that I really didn't want to talk to him because I was afraid I'd give away the surprise.

I thought of leaving home for a few days, but I figured that might make him more suspicious, so I stayed and tried to talk as little as possible. (no easy job for me!)

The big plan was to surprise Scotty when he got home from work. I would tell him that one of his presents arrived early and the girls and I were so excited we wanted to give it to him.

He sat down on the bar stool and closed his eyes. Dennis and Sue quietly came into the room. Dennis leaned over his shoulder and whispered something in his ear.

Scotty had a puzzled expression on his face as he opened his eyes. He turned his head slightly and for a few seconds didn't move. He seemed almost disoriented. Sue started laughing and he jumped off the stool so fast it fell to the floor. He tried to hug them both at once.

We had accomplished our goal. He was surprised!

The next few days were perfect. Scotty and Dennis wanted to do their own things (go air boating, go to the pawn shops), while Sue and I wanted to do our own things (shop and talk and talk and shop). In the evenings we all went out to dinner.

Those dinners were déjà vue times from our college days. Of course, now we could actually afford a sit down restaurant compared to fast food, but that didn't really matter. What mattered was the company. We laughed so hard our sides hurt and at times the tea threatened to come out our noses. We had several tables giving us stares, but we didn't care. We were enjoying ourselves and for a brief time all our cares and worries were forgotten and we were just four close friends who seemed twenty years younger.

When we got home after dinner, we had a rousing game of Spades going. It was the girls versus the guys and naturally we girls won (no mercy to the birthday boy).

We laughed some more and it got to the point where our teenager groggily walked out of her room and exclaimed, "Boy, you all are loud!"

If we passed the sound barrier of a teenager we knew we must be making some serious noise. We didn't stop. It was our weekend and we were enjoying it.

The only bad thing about good times is it seems they end so quickly. Ours came to a close on Sunday morning as we waited at the airport.

How do you explain to two people, who in some ways are closer than family, that you are so glad they came? That they were the only ones who could have pulled this birthday surprise off. That you wish they lived closer so you could get together more often.

We all hugged and said our good-byes.

What I really wanted to say was:

Thank you, thank you for shelling out hundreds of dollars of your hard earned money to fly down and help me surprise Scotty. Thank you for putting up with us all these years and still loving us despite all our flaws. Thank you for always being there when we needed you.

Thank you for giving us the greatest gift of all—your friendship.

A TALE OF TWO PURSES

The sea shells first caught my eye. It seemed as if they covered the whole purse. I knew this was the right gift for Mother's Day. After all, my mother had been hinting for a new purse for weeks and I had enough money saved to buy this one.

I felt very grown up as the cashier placed the purse in a bag and handed it to me. My daddy told me to think of a good hiding place so my mother wouldn't find her present. I told him I knew the perfect place.

On our way home I took the purse out of the bag for another look. It was so pretty! It was a tan, straw purse about ten inches by fourteen inches with a small straw handle. The inside was lined with a tan material a shade lighter than the outside. The front—oh, the front was just gorgeous! Sea shells in all shapes and sizes covered most of it with small green bows in the corners.

Of course, what's beautiful to an eight-year-old child may sometimes seem gaudy to an adult.

My brother (who was older and wealthier) also decided to give my mother a purse that year. He decided to give Mother her present early.

I will never forget the hurt and despair I felt as I watched her open that gift. Out of the box came a beautiful white leather purse with lots of compartments that Mother was oohing and ahhing over. 'How did my brother know she needed a purse? This was just too expensive! He shouldn't have!'

Well, she got that one right, I thought. He sure shouldn't have!

Then she spoke the final blow, "This is the most beautiful purse I've ever seen."

That did it! I did what any other eight-year-old would do when faced with a tough situation—I cried.

Everyone stopped and stared at me.

"Why, what's the matter, honey?" my mother asked.

"You love his present more than mine!"

With that proclamation I ran to my room and threw myself on the bed to cry some more. My mother came in, closed the door, and sat down beside me. "Now Debbie, what's this all about?"

I was beginning to feel bad for making such a scene, but I couldn't forget those words, "...most beautiful purse I've ever seen." There was no way she was ever going to carry my purse. I sat up, rubbed my eyes, and pointed to the closet.

"What's in there?" my mother asked.

I got up from the bed, opened the closet, and from beneath a pile of clothes I got the carefully wrapped purse. Hesitantly, I handed it to my mother.

"Do you want me to open this now?"

I nodded yes.

I watched as she tore off the wrapping paper and looked inside the box. Her eyes widened in surprise and she exclaimed, "Oh honey, this is the most beautiful purse I've ever seen!"

She gave me a big hug and kiss before I could tell her that she told my brother the same thing only minutes before.

"Oh, I know it is," Mother said, "and I meant every word. Jerry's purse *was* the most beautiful I'd ever seen until I saw yours. You see, men don't always know what to look for in a purse, probably because they don't carry them. The white purse is certainly pretty, but it will get dirty easily because of the color and then with all those compartments I won't be able to find a thing.

"But this purse," and she held it up and twirled it around, "this purse is good for every day of the week. It's nice and roomy and I'll be able to put everything I need in there. I don't want to hurt your brother's feelings, so please don't tell him I said any of this. I'll carry your purse first and then I'll carry his, OK?"

I nodded my consent and gave my mother a big hug. My mother carried my purse every single day until it practically fell apart (which only took a couple of months). She would proudly hold the purse up when we met some of her friends and let them know it was a special Mother's Day gift from me. I would beam as they complimented Mother on such a lovely purse.

Looking back, I'm not sure if she told them because she was so proud of it or because she wanted to make sure they knew she didn't pick it out! It was probably a little of both.

That Mother's Day was so long ago and there were many in between that I have no recollection of at all. Yet it is that particular Mother's Day that I will always remember. It's when I learned some valuable lessons about motherhood that I didn't realize until I had children of my own: a mother can make any situation better, a mother can play both sides of the fence so each child will feel like number one, and a mother will always love any gift that a child gives and exclaim, "This is the most beautiful gift I've ever seen"—and mean every word.

FATHER'S DAY

I stood in front of the display for a good five minutes before I admitted defeat. I was never going to find it. It being the perfect Father's Day card for my daddy.

There were many cards from which to choose. Some were humorous, some were sentimental, but none of them said exactly what I was feeling.

Every year I go through the same ritual—looking for the perfect card, never finding it, but finding something close, signing my name and dropping it in the mail.

Why can't I find the perfect card? Why can't I find a card that will say 'thank you for being both a dad AND a mom to me'? Why can't I find the words to express how I really feel to the man who is responsible for my being here?

I believe it's because we have such a unique relationship. We started out with the normal daddy-daughter roles, but that all changed when my mother died. Suddenly we were thrown together, the two of us, alone in the house we once thought of as home, but now with a terrible void in it. We were both missing my mother and we didn't know how to console each other. I only had to deal with my hurt; my daddy had to deal with mine plus his own.

My daddy threw himself into his work and I threw myself into after school activities. We tried to have dinner together, but since my mother had been the cook in the family, we often ate sandwiches or take-out. The few times I tried to cook, my daddy never said a negative word about the almost black pork chops or the hamburgers that were so hard they could pass for Frisbees. He always ate whatever I fixed and thanked me. He knew I was trying.

The only advice my daddy ever gave me in the kitchen was to make sure I rinsed all the soap off the dishes or we'd get "the back door trots."

While Daddy was short on kitchen advice, he certainly wasn't lacking in other areas.

Homework papers had to pass inspection by Daddy. He would always ask, "Is this your best work? Is this your neatest handwriting?"

I would reluctantly take the paper back and do it over mumbling the whole time. I didn't realize that Daddy was teaching me a valuable lesson—"anything worth doing is worth doing right"—even homework!

During college I'd come home and whine that I couldn't find a job on campus to fit in with my schedule. Daddy gave me the same advice every time, "the squeaky wheel gets the oil" and "persistence pays." I took Daddy's advice and I got a job.

After my older daughter was born, Daddy stopped by to see us one morning. As I related how many times I'd been up and down during the night with her, Daddy just smiled and said, "You pay for your raisin' when you have children of your own." Well, my raisin' must have cost a pretty penny!

When my husband got a job nine hundred miles from our hometown, it was hard to say good-bye to Daddy. As usual, he had some words of advice. He smiled at me and said, "Things have a way of working out for the best. You'll be fine."

It's been eleven years since we've moved. Things have worked out rather nicely, but I do miss seeing Daddy.

During the years we've been apart, we've had weekly phone conversations and yearly visits. Each visit has a ritual ending. There is a teary good-bye on my part and the same farewell, "I wish we had more time to spend."

There is a big hug from Daddy and the same advice every year, "Well, time marches on."

He's right, as usual. Time *is* marching on, but I would like to find a Father's Day card to make it stop—just for a little while. A card that would stop time while I try to tell my daddy thanks for everything and I love you.

APPRECIATING AUTUMN

A four day weekend in the middle of October could only mean one thing—throw caution to the wind and head for the hills—which is exactly what we did.

Autumn is the time of year I miss most in Virginia. Watching the leaves change from green to brilliant shades of red and gold, feeling the crispness in the air, and listening to the leaves crunch beneath my feet. It is also the time of year that I want to share my memories of autumns passed with my daughters. What better way than to actually take them back and let them bask in the glory of those ole' mountains, but some things are just not meant to be.

I knew we were in trouble before we backed out of the garage and both girls wanted the same seat in our mini-van.

Now, I took a friend's advice and didn't have more

children than car windows, yet both daughters wanted the same seat when they had five from which to choose. It was decided that age ruled. Ginny gloated and Megan pouted.

The rest of the trip up was rather pleasant considering we drove all night. As we were going over the mountain into Erwin, Tennessee in the wee hours of the morning, the headlights shone against some trees along the road. I saw a flash of orange. "Oh, look, the leaves have turned."

Ginny peered out the window and in her best teenage, nonchalant way, responded, "They look kinda burnt to me."

"Go back to sleep. They'll look better in the daylight," I promised.

Oh, and they did! Glorious colors of red, orange, and gold mixed with the green. When the sun shone on them in the early morning light it was breathtaking!

"Just smell that crisp, mountain air," I instructed as we all piled out of the van at Dennis and Sue's house.

"Personally, I'd rather smell MALL air," Ginny added.

"Don't get smart," I warned.

"Mom, I didn't mean anything, it's just that I can't see how you and Daddy can get so excited about a place that doesn't have a mall within fifty miles."

"Hey, Norton has a twenty-four hour Wal-Mart. What more do you need?"

The eyes were beginning to roll and the generation gap was beginning to widen, but maybe I could get some appreciation for the mountains before we left.

By Thursday afternoon Megan and her friend, Marcy, were having the time of their lives playing in the leaves while Ginny and her friend, Leigha, stayed inside looking through magazines and painting their nails.

I looked at my husband and asked, "Do you think Ginny has even noticed that it's autumn here?"

He looked at me and smiled, "Did you ever notice autumn when you were fourteen?"

I was surrounded by smart-alecks.

Friday evening Sue suggested taking all the girls to a football game. Wonderful! Now Ginny and Megan would finally experience REAL football weather. I bundled Megan up so much that she could hardly move. Ginny wanted no part of wearing a jacket. By the end of the evening no one had on a jacket and Ginny wore an "I-told you-so" look, but she had the good sense not to say anything.

Saturday brought cloudy skies and a hint of rain. We were all going to the big craft show at Mountain Empire Community College. I was excitedly telling the girls about seeing people make apple cider, lye soap, corn meal, and our all time favorite—apple butter!

"Doesn't Pappy make his apple butter in the crock pot?" Megan asked.

"Yes, but you're going to see how people made it BEFORE they had crock pots. With an open fire and a big kettle..."

Megan interrupted, "I think I like Pappy's way better."

Appreciating heritage days was proving to be difficult.

That evening we were all standing around in the kitchen and I was complaining to Sue that Ginny and Megan would never really experience autumn except the few times we were able to make it back.

"That's not true," Ginny piped up. "I know what autumn is—it's about two degrees cooler than summer, you sweat like crazy, and you can still wear shorts to the football games! That's our autumn."

I stood there a moment just looking at her. She was right.

♥ KWITCHYERBELLYAKIN ♥

My memories of autumn will always be the crisp, mountain air and the beautiful foliage, while Ginny and Megan will remember the warm breezes and the palm trees.

One memory is no better than the other—just different. While I was trying to make them appreciate the beauty of my memories, I failed to see the beauty in theirs.

A SENTIMENTAL COOK

With the holidays fast approaching, every good cook is going through the recipe box to find the old favorites and maybe try a few new ones.

I was going to do that—once. That's before I decided that recipe cards were cold, unemotional, and they didn't bring any good memories to mind. What? You thought recipes were just a place to list ingredients and give instructions? Then you have much to learn. When used properly, recipes not only make wonderful things to eat, they make wonderful memories as well. Let me explain.

Three years ago I decided to organize my recipe file. Actually, it was a recipe MESS with papers stuck in cookbooks, envelopes, and drawers. This was no small task I was about to undertake. I began by dumping everything on the dining room table and warning my family that they might not see the table or me for days. When I was finished I would be the most efficient, most organized cook on the block. WRONG!

My high hopes began to unravel that first day when I began going through my recipe envelope, a catch all for recipes given to me over the years. I couldn't bear to part with my dear, deceased Aunt Ida's handwritten recipe for zucchini bread. It was written on a page torn from a desk calendar— Tuesday, December 28, 1976. Yes, I remembered. My husband and I had only been married three months. We were in for the Christmas holidays visiting relatives. When we visited Aunt Ida, she made the zucchini bread for us. I loved the bread and asked for the recipe. She was so pleased that we liked it that she wrote the recipe on the closest paper she could find. I was now holding that paper in my hands. Did I want to rewrite it on a card so it could be neat and fit into a file box? Or did I want to leave it exactly as it was so every time I made the recipe I could remember that day and my Aunt Ida? I left it alone.

Next, I took out a newspaper page with the headline "Main Dishes for Four Under $5." I laughed and laughed. This one was really old! It was left over from my college days when my roommates and I decided we'd cook more economical and nutritious meals. That thought lasted about one day. We did, however, make one of the recipes listed—Hobo Meatball Stew. I think the name pretty well summed up our feelings on that one! I decided to keep this page because it would always be good for a laugh.

A quiche recipe written on a folded envelope took me back many years. I was standing in the kitchen of our first home in Virginia talking on the phone. My infant daughter was sleeping in my arms as I took down the recipe from my friend's mother. I didn't want to wake my daughter so I wrote the recipe on the first thing I could find—an old envelope. Most people would just see an old, worn envelope when they looked at my quiche recipe, but I saw much more. I saw my daughter as a baby again, smelling fresh and sweet from a bath and sleeping gently on my shoulder. I left the old worn envelope just as it was.

Hot mushroom turnovers, now that's a little appetizer to make anyone's mouth water. I don't like mushrooms, but I loved this recipe. Why? Because it was the only thing that I ever made that looked exactly like the picture. When I saw this recipe torn from a magazine it gave me confidence. It would not give me confidence on a neat little card.

Finally, I started getting into the real "meat" of the recipes, desserts! I looked at the recipe for orange crunch cake written on stationery from my mother-in-law. She made the cake once and so did I. Once was enough. It was one of the best cakes I ever tasted, but it took all day to make! I decided I'd keep this recipe as it was because it reminded me that I once had enough patience to bake all day.

My eyes caught sight of another magazine page and I was almost afraid to look. Could it be? Yes, this was the mother of all desserts. This was "The Perfect Chocolate Cake" complete with pictures and step by step instructions! It was torn from an old *McCall's* dated October 1982. I remembered the first time I laid eyes on this delicious looking confection. I called the one person who appreciated chocolate as much as I did—my sister-in-law, Alice Marie. We promised each other we would make it the next time we got together. It's been over ten years and we've gotten together plenty of times, but that cake hasn't been made. I decided I couldn't part with this page because it reminded me of promises to keep. Besides, the picture alone looked good enough to eat!

I was reaching for another recipe when my husband walked in the door.

"Honey, I thought you were going to get organized. What happened?"

"Well, I've decided there's more to recipes than mere words. There are memories, there are goals to reach, there are..."

He was beginning to look at me funny. "I just want to know what's for dinner."

"There's only one thing to make when I have a mess like this —RESERVATIONS!"

P.S. I still have my recipe mess AND my memories.

A CHRISTMAS WISH FOR TEACHERS

Bradley raised his hand to signal for silence. There was a sudden hush as all the third-grade children in room 305 at Lockmar Elementary School anxiously waited for Mrs. Benton.

I happened to be in the pod that day volunteering with Apple Corps. I knew Mrs. Benton ran a tight ship, but this class was REALLY quiet!

Mrs. Benton came in the pod, looked through the glass window at her perfect classroom, smiled at me and said, "Today is Raffle Day."

Ah, the legendary raffle! Mrs. Benton is famous around Lockmar for her raffles. Younger children want to know what they're all about and older children want to know if she's still having them.

I understood the basics of the raffle. Children receive a ticket for good work or behavior. They write their name on the back of the ticket and save it in their desk until it's time for a raffle. The class as a whole must earn the raffle. They must exhibit good behavior and manners in line, in the cafeteria, and in their special classes. If they do all this, they earn a letter beginning with the letter "R". When they've earned all six letters, then they've earned THE RAFFLE!

Understanding the basics of the raffle was one thing; understanding the impact it had on the children was quite another.

When Mrs. Benton walked in with that special raffle box in her hands, I was witness to a small miracle. All the children in that classroom had smiles on their faces. They were so excited and happy that their little bodies were twitching in their chairs, but not one child dared to get up because they knew the rules.

As Mrs. Benton held up the first item, a friendship bracelet, and announced who received it, every child clapped and smiled as if their own name had been called. This went on for about thirty minutes. An item held up (such as bouncing balls, coloring books, yo-yos), a name called (Franklin, Rhia, Nathaniel...), and twenty-three children looking as excited for the person receiving the prize as if they had received it themselves.

I forgot the work, I forgot the time, but I sure didn't forget what I was seeing. For I was seeing every mother's dream; children looking so happy, children showing their manners, children being respectful, not just to the teacher, but also to each other.

Mrs. Benton's professional title is not miracle worker, but it is synonymous—she is a teacher. A teacher who truly enjoys what she does and it shows on the faces of her students.

She is a teacher who wants to challenge her children and she has a class of children who want to be challenged. She is a teacher who arrives early, stays late and pays for most school supplies out of her own pocket.

What a wonderful present we parents have received from the teachers of Brevard County. They have given our children their time and their talent to help them become better students and better citizens.

My Christmas wish for Mrs. Benton, and for all the other caring teachers in Brevard County, is that the School Board will recognize what we as a community already know: Our teachers are the greatest. Let's pay them accordingly!

PAT'S PRESENTS

"Has the package come yet?" Megan asks breathlessly as she gets off her bike in the driveway.

"No, not yet, but I'm sure it will be here soon."

"Well, Christmas is getting pretty close. I can't wait to see what Pat sends this year. I just love her presents, don't you Mommy?"

"Yes, sweetie. I love her presents."

I do love her presents, but what I, and the rest of my family, love even more is the way we *receive* the presents.

Pat is my cousin who travels quite a bit and always manages to find us unique gifts. She is organized and efficient —except when it comes to wrapping Christmas presents.

The first Christmas we noticed she was slipping I was pregnant with Megan. My first gift was a beautiful maternity dress. The second gift was an ironing board cover. Now Pat knows that I don't iron, but I thought she might be throwing me a hint. The last gift was a lovely red blouse, but definitely not my size, maternity or not.

My husband opened one of his gifts. It was a blue nursing gown.

He peered through the openings in the front as he said, "I think this one is for you."

Ginny received, along with other gifts, a man's shirt that we decided must have been meant for my husband, but then we weren't sure.

I called the next day and she explained that the ironing board cover was meant for her mom and the red blouse was meant for a friend. She wasn't sure who got my other gift.

I told her not to worry because she had added some real mystery to our gift exchange.

One year I opened a gift from Pat's husband (at least that's what was written on the tag). Inside was a pair of lacy, bikini panties.

"Oh," I said, "I sure hope she made a mistake on this one."

My husband asked, "Just how well do you know Pat's husband?"

"Not this well," I told him.

Ginny and Megan thought it was hilarious.

When Pat received the thank-you note that Christmas she called and between fits of laughter she managed to get out, "Those panties were from me! I got the tags mixed up!"

This past Christmas the gifts were the most mysterious of all.

The packages arrived early...strange.

I opened one box to find several small gifts inside without any name tags. There was something else in the bottom.

"Pat probably put these in by mistake," Ginny said as she held up scissors and tape. "I bet she wonders where this stuff is."

I wondered if she had even missed it yet.

The next box contained presents of all sizes and shapes. As I took the first brightly-wrapped one out, Megan asked, "Whose is that?"

I looked on the tag and said, "Well, Megan I think this one is for Ginny, but as you know, we can never be sure."

As Megan took the present to place under the tree, she turned it over and exclaimed, "This one is for me. It has MY name on it!"

She handed the package back to me and, sure enough, there was Megan's name taped to the bottom while Ginny's name was taped to the top!

"Hmm...let's see what else is in the box," I told her, not wanting to think about trying to decide who would open *that* present!

As we took out all the gifts, we made a startling discovery—no other gift had a name tag! All the tags had fallen to the bottom of the box!

"Mom, how do we know who gets what gift?" Ginny asked.

"I think I'll call Pat now and ask her that very question."

Pat, as usual, had a solution to the problem. "Have everyone pick out a gift to open. If it doesn't fit or they don't like it, just give it to someone else."

We had a great time opening those presents. It was so much fun to peek inside the box and then make everyone guess whose gift was inside—except for the cookie canisters.

Pat sent us several canisters of cookies made in Old Salem (they weren't wrapped and they didn't have a name on them). After opening two of the canisters and eating the delicious gingersnap cookies inside, I decided to save the third canister for my in-laws.

When we went to their house on Christmas morning I took the canister of cookies. After dinner, while everyone was sitting around the table, I asked Ginny to open the cookies and put them on a plate. She took the lid off, looked inside, and then looked at me.

"Mom, I don't think you want me to put this on a plate."

"Ginny, just put them on the plate. It's simple enough."

"O.K., but remember you made me."

Ginny slowly pulled the slinkiest, sexiest, nightgown out of the canister.

Everyone stared for a moment and then my husband mumbled, "Those are some cookies!"

I'm glad I have a good relationship with my in-laws.

After that episode I almost bought Pat some stick-on name tags, but I decided against it. She probably would forget where she put them and if she did find them, she'd probably stick them on the wrong present. Besides, it's a lot more fun wondering what she'll come up with from year to year.

However, I have decided to check all cookie canisters before leaving home.

A SPECIAL SANTA

"Oh, look Mommy. Here he is."

Megan lifts the tissue wrapped object from the box and places it gently on my lap. We look at each other and smile as I unfold the tissue. TA-DA! Santa-the tree-topper!

Poor Santa—he has seen better days. None of us mind, though. He's ours, and he has a special place on our tree and in our hearts.

"Mommy, after Daddy puts him on the tree, will you tell us the story about how you found him?"

"Of course, it wouldn't be Christmas without the Santa story."

Decorating the tree is a big event in our home, but before that begins, we have an even bigger event: placing Santa ceremoniously on top of the tree (this job can be done only by my husband) followed by telling the history of our Santa (which can be done only by me).

As my husband puts Santa reverently on top there is silence, but once he's in place we all cheer. It's now time for the story. Ginny and Megan settle themselves on the sofa and look at me as if I'm about to tell them something for the first time. Even my husband sits down to listen (to make sure I tell it right). I look at my family. It's probably the most attentive they've been all year, and the funny thing is they know this story by heart.

"Go on Mommy, tell us." Megan is becoming impatient.

"Many years ago, when Daddy and I got married, we went to a town called Gatlinburg for our honeymoon."

"We've been there haven't we, Mommy?"

"Shh, let Mom finish."

"Yes, we've all been there. Now this town had a wonderful Christmas shop with the most beautiful decorations you've ever seen. Daddy and I decided that we wanted to get something special for our first Christmas together, something we could keep for a long time. We looked for HOURS."

At this point my husband nods his head in agreement and the girls laugh.

"We looked at ornaments, but none of them spoke to us and said, 'Buy me, buy me'. We looked at tree skirts, but they just weren't right. We were almost ready to give up when we spotted a shelf of tree toppers. Oh, they were gorgeous! The angels had beautiful wings with soft glittering dresses and the stars were shining with such warm colors. We were just standing there taking in all the beauty of those tree toppers when our eyes looked in the corner, and there he was. Poor Santa. He wasn't fancy. He didn't glow. He just sat there.

"Standing about ten inches tall he was made of burlap. He had a deep red hat with the seam going down the front.

Straw made the tassel of his hat. His coat was also the same deep red with white rick-rack on the front. The ends of his sleeves were made of straw, and the edge of his coat had a band of straw around it. He had no arms. His face was brown burlap with black felt eyes shaped like little quarter moons. His nose was a bright red bead with straw sticking out from either end to be his moustache.

"His hair and beard were all straw. He seemed sadly out of place next to all the glitter and glamour of the other tree toppers. He had a certain quality, a one-of-a-kind quality. He seemed to speak to us: 'Please take me home. I may not be fancy on the outside, but I'm a good Santa. I have a kind heart. I'll watch over your tree'.

"We both looked at each other and we knew. We knew this Santa was the special Christmas decoration we had been hoping to find. We knew it even more when we asked the clerk to take it down and she made a comment about how long the store had had him. I told her he was just waiting for the right people to come along.

"That first year that Santa was on our tree one of our neighbors came over and said, 'Nice tree, but where did you get that ugly Santa?'

"Well, I told him off right then and there. Remember, girls, some people only notice what is on the outside.

"Santa has been on our tree all these years. He may not be the prettiest or the fanciest, but he's special, and that's what matters."

That's the end of the story, and yet it isn't, really. It's a story that will be told every year with something added or something taken away. If not by me, then by Ginny or Megan. It's tradition.

"Mommy, tell us the story about the elf now."

I smile and begin, "Do you see that little red elf sitting in the tree branches? Many years ago, when I was just a little girl..."

Another story—another tradition. I hope you all keep your traditions this holiday season. Merry Christmas!

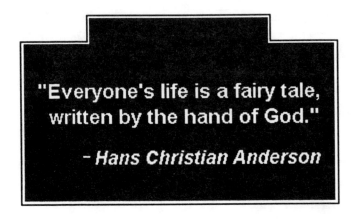

"Everyone's life is a fairy tale, written by the hand of God."

- Hans Christian Anderson

THE SISTERS THREE

The angel looked puzzled as she glanced at the list of impending births.

"God, I don't mean to question Your judgment, but I see here that one baby girl is about to be born on December 4, 1954, in a little place called Indian Creek."

"Yes, that's correct."

"But God, I see that You don't plan on giving her any sisters."

"That is correct."

The angel bit her lower lip as she looked down at the massive book and then back to God. She spoke in a soft voice, "God, I believe You're making a mistake with this one. I see that in 1971 You plan to call her mother home. Her brother will be coming home shortly after. Her daddy will be working long hours at his job. She needs a sister."

The angel braced herself for the fury that she was sure would follow, but God only looked at her and smiled.

"No, I have not made a mistake. Her mother's

homecoming will be difficult to accept, but she will manage. And yes, you are right; she will need some sisters, but not necessarily ones that live with her."

The angel looked startled. "I don't understand."

"Look in the years 1945, 1947 and 1958. Don't you see three sisters being born on Indian Creek?"

"Yes God, but what does that have to do with this baby girl?"

"It has everything to do with her. The three sisters will be more than just cousins; they will become the sisters that she so desperately needs.

"When she no longer has her mother on earth she will have reminders of her mother in the three sisters."

"How can that be?"

"From the oldest sister she will receive the gift of thoughtfulness. I've made sure the oldest has the same quality that her mother possessed. The oldest sister will also nurture her and give her much needed guidance.

"From the middle sister she will receive the gift of compassion. She will learn to look beyond physical appearance and straight into a person's heart. She will hurt when others hurt and rejoice when others are happy.

"From the youngest sister she will receive the gift of a free spirit. She will learn that it's fine to follow the beat of a different drummer whether it's in fashion or in friendship. She will learn to appreciate art from the youngest."

"But God, I still don't understand. When will they become sisters?"

"Ah, their sisterhood will grow each year as they grow. They will love each other, sacrifice for each other, and always be aware of the needs of each other. They will be sisters in their hearts and that's all that really matters."

And, so it was, as the angel closed the massive book, that she had a smile on her face knowing that the sisters three would indeed become ... the sisters four!

BEGINNINGS AND ENDINGS

We had decided to walk a little longer than usual. The night air felt cool after such a humid, fall day.

As we stopped at the intersection, my husband turned to me and said, "I think you should write a book."

"I think you're crazy," I said. I thought he'd been doing too much yard work in the hot sun.

"No, I'm serious."

"So am I. Do you know what's involved in writing a book? Do you know how much time it takes? Do you..."

He put his fingers to my lips. "You *can* do it. I believe in you."

"That's all well and good, but your believing in me will not get a book written."

"Maybe, but your believing in yourself will."

I stared at him. He was serious!

"What kind of book did you have in mind?" I asked.

"Those little stories you write would make a good book. People could read one or two while they're in the bathroom."

Somehow, I had imagined my first book in a sacred spot on someone's coffee table or possibly someone's night stand, but on the back of someone's toilet?! No thanks.

Over the next few weeks the idea began to take root and I decided to give it a try (back of the toilet seat and all).

My husband was constantly giving me encouragement. He even suggested that my writing might help finance our daughters' education.

I think our visions were a little different on exactly *how* I could help them. He envisioned cold, hard cash while I envisioned an education at the School of Hard Knocks.

"Girls," I would say, "if you want to go to college then you better help me sell these eight hundred books sitting in our living room."

So much for financing their college education.

My husband was not the only one giving me encouragement. Family and friends were also supportive. The most unusual encouragement, however, came from a stranger who had no idea how much she helped me.

One morning, nearing the completion of this book, I got up at 5 a.m. with a knot in my stomach and a feeling of panic. I stared at a blank page for almost an hour. Negative thoughts started filling my mind.

Why in the world was I doing this? What made me think I could write a book? I couldn't even finish the story I was working on, much less a book.

It was a gloom and doom Monday morning. Since I was getting nowhere with my book, I decided to do something constructive: laundry.

As I started to hang the sheets on the line, one dropped to the ground.

"Great," I thought, "Murphy's Law strikes again."

I put the dirty sheet back in the washer and took the second load of clothes to the line.

This time I dropped two towels. It was not my day. I almost said some choice words that my husband uses when he does woodworking, but I didn't. I only thought them.

As I carried the basket with the now dirty towels back to the house the phone rang.

I usually screen the calls with the answering machine, but I was in such a foul mood that I picked up the phone and in a less-than-pleasant voice I barked, " Hello!"

There was a slight pause and then a woman's voice asked, "Is this Debbie Pender.... Pendergrass?"

"Oh terrific," I thought, "I've answered the phone for a sales pitch!"

"Pendergast," I corrected.

"Is this the Debbie Pendergast that wrote "Kwitchyerbellyakin" for the newspaper?"

I dropped the basket of clothes. The music from "The Twilight Zone" started running through my mind.

That article appeared in our local paper over a year ago. Why would this woman be calling me now? TODAY?

I finally managed to stammer that I was Debbie Pendergast.

"My name is Rose and I've been meaning to call you for some time. I wanted to tell you how much that article meant to me. I also wanted to tell you that because you took the time to write it, I took the time to make several Kwitchyerbellyakin samplers and send them to friends across the country. Thank you for sharing that wonderful story about the sampler."

"Oh, thank you for calling. You'll never know how much it means to me."

Rose would never understand that by a simple phone call at just the right time she had pulled me out of a slump. She had given me the encouragement I needed—the kindness of a stranger.

From the complaining of a teenager, to the despair of a newly planted Floridian, to the panicking of a wannabe writer, the little Kwitchyerbellyakin sampler has always seemed to enter my life when I need it the most.

Coincidence? Maybe, but I like to think my mother has a hand in it somehow.

About the Author:

Debbie Pendergast grew up in the mountains of southwestern Virginia. A graduate of East Tennessee State University in Johnson City, Tennessee, she now lives in Palm Bay, Florida, with her husband, two daughters, one iguana, one hamster, and one fat cat.

About the illustrator:

Jaynie Gibson lives in Charlotte, North Carolina with her Pekinese, 'Pudgie', her wonderful roommate, Julie, and Julie's Schnauzer, 'Max'.

She illustrated this book as a lifetime favor to her cousin and expects payment for many years to come.

To order additional copies of **Kwitchyerbellyakin**, complete the information below.

Ship to: (please print)

Name _____

Address _____

City, State, Zip _____

Day phone _____

_____ copies of *Kwitchyerbellyakin* @ $6.95 each $_____

S & H @ $2.25 for 1st book to same address ($1 each additional) $_____

Florida residents add 6% tax $_____

Total amount enclosed $_____

*Make checks payable to **Debbie Pendergast***

Send to: Debbie Pendergast
P.O. Box 500192 • Malabar, FL 32950-0192

To order additional copies of **Kwitchyerbellyakin**, complete the information below.

Ship to: (please print)

Name _____

Address _____

City, State, Zip _____

Day phone _____

_____ copies of *Kwitchyerbellyakin* @ $6.95 each $_____

S & H @ $2.25 for 1st book to same address ($1 each additional) $_____

Florida residents add 6% tax $_____

Total amount enclosed $_____

*Make checks payable to **Debbie Pendergast***

Send to: Debbie Pendergast
P.O. Box 500192 • Malabar, FL 32950-0192